HOW'S YOUR HEALTH?

Tooth Decay

Angela Royston

W

FRANKLIN WATTS

First published in 2006 by
Franklin Watts
338 Euston Road
London NW1 3BH

Franklin Watts Australia
Hachette Children's Books
Level 17/207 Kent Street
Sydney NSW 2000

Produced by Calcium, New Brook House, 385 Alfreton Road, Nottingham, NG7 5LR

Editor: Sarah Eason
Design: Paul Myerscough
Illustration: Annie Boberg and Geoff Ward
Picture research: Sarah Jameson
Consultant: Dr Stephen Earwicker

Acknowledgements:
The publisher would like to thank the following for permission to reproduce photographs:
Alamy p.6, p.9, p.10, p.11, p.13, p.15, p.19, p.27; Science Photo Library p.18; Inmagine
p.7, p.16; Tudor Photography p.21; Chris Fairclough Photography p.17, p.20, p.22, p.24,
p.25, p.26.

Every attempt has been made to clear copyright. Should there be any inadvertent omission
please apply to the publisher for rectification.

A CIP catalogue record for this book is available from the British Library.

Dewey Decimal Classification Number: 617.6'3

ISBN-10: 0 7496 6670 6
ISBN-13: 978 0 7496 6670 5

Printed in China

Franklin Watts is a division of Hachette Children's Books.

Contents

What is tooth decay?   6

What are teeth made of?   8

What causes tooth decay?   10

What happens when a tooth decays?   12

How do dentists treat tooth decay?   14

How can you stop tooth decay?   16

What is gum disease?   18

How is gum disease treated?   20

How can you prevent gum disease?   22

Which foods and drinks harm teeth?   24

Which foods and drink are good for teeth?   26

Glossary   28

Find out more   29

Index   30

What is tooth decay?

If someone gets a hole in their tooth it is called tooth decay.

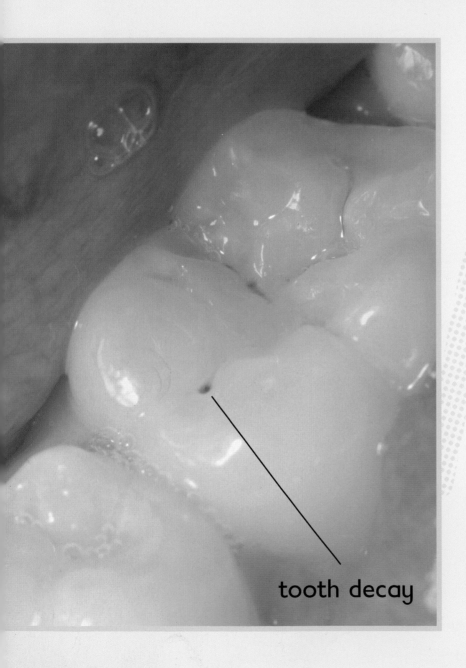

tooth decay

Tooth decay begins as a small hole on the surface of a tooth. If the decay is not treated, the hole will get bigger and bigger. The tooth will then begin to hurt.

Tooth decay

If a tooth hurts all the time, it may have tooth decay. These things may make your teeth hurt for a minute or two, but don't mean you have tooth decay:

✚ Drinking hot or cold drinks.
✚ Eating hot or cold food.
✚ Breathing in cold air.
✚ Brushing teeth.
✚ Eating sweets.

It is important to look after your teeth and keep them healthy. Healthy teeth help you to chew food. They also look good when you smile!

What are teeth made of?

Most of your tooth is made of a hard material called **dentine**. Dentine is covered with an even harder material, called **enamel**.

The outside of a tooth is the hardest part of the body. However, the centre of a tooth is soft. It is filled with blood and **nerves**.

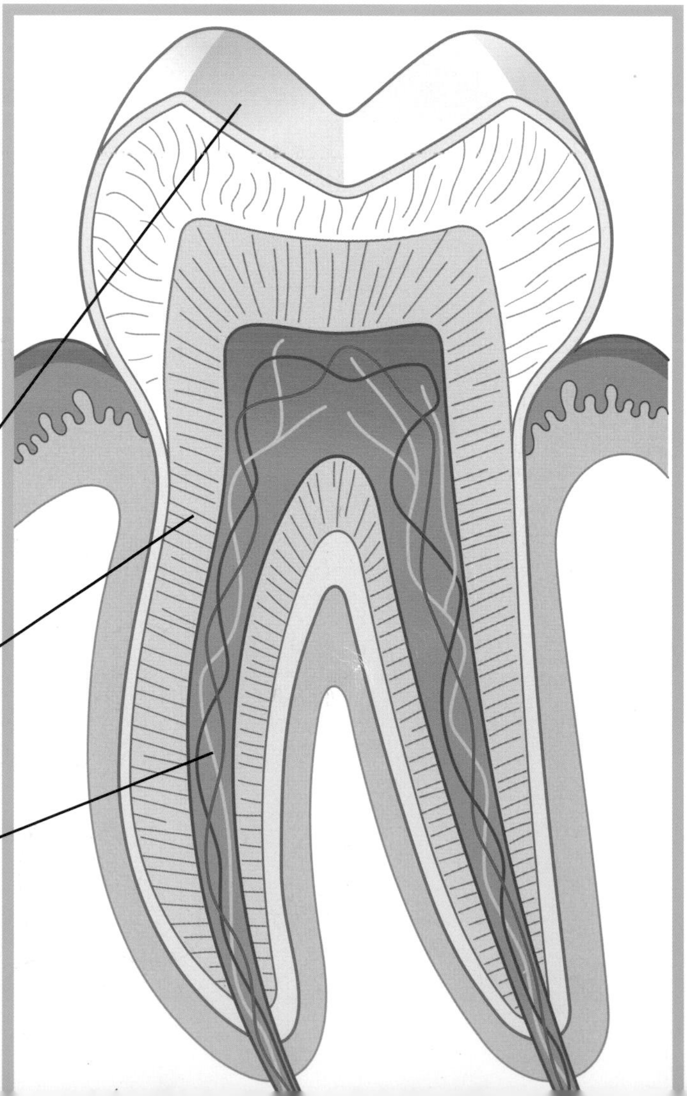

enamel

dentine

blood and nerves

Teeth are made in the **gums**. People are born with two sets of teeth, which are buried in their gums. The first set, called milk teeth, grow through the gums when you are about six months old. They fall out as the second set, called adult teeth, begin to grow through the gums.

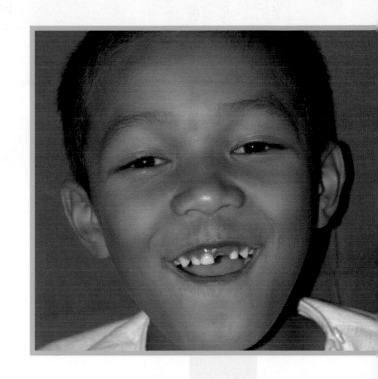

Teeth shapes

+ Front teeth are flat and sharp. They are called **incisors** and bite into food. There are four at the top and four at the bottom of your mouth.

+ At either side of the front teeth are four pointed teeth, called **canines**. They tear off mouthfuls of food.

+ Back teeth are large and flat. They are called **premolars** and **molars**. They chew food into mushy pieces.

What causes tooth decay?

Sugar in food or drink turns into an **acid** in your mouth. The acid can burn a hole in your tooth. This is the start of tooth decay.

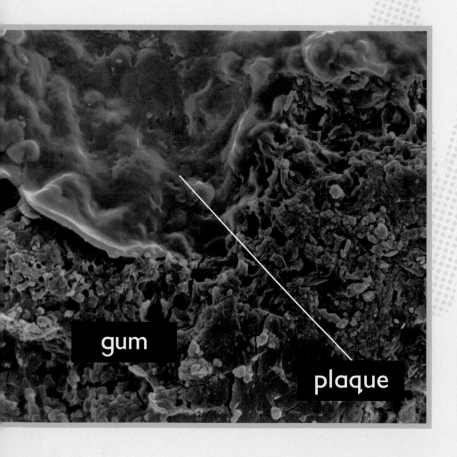

gum

plaque

Plaque is a sticky paste that is found on teeth. Plaque is made by tiny living things called **bacteria**. This photograph has been specially coloured. It has also been **magnified** so the plaque looks bigger than it really is.

Try this!

Suck a **disclosure tablet** when you have cleaned your teeth and you will see just how clean your teeth really are! Brush your teeth afterwards until they are white again.

The bacteria in plaque feed on sugar that clings to teeth. Plaque contains an acid that can make holes in teeth. The plaque in this photograph has been dyed pink by a disclosure tablet.

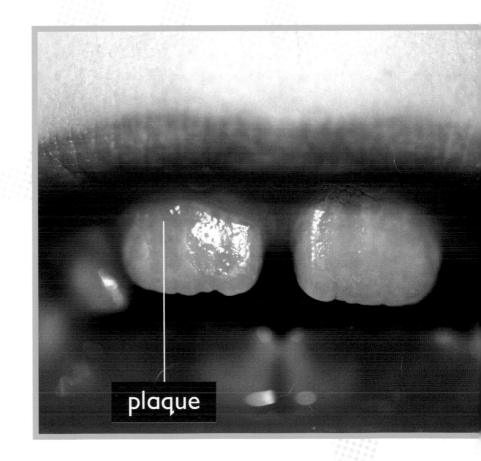

plaque

What happens when a tooth decays?

If tooth decay reaches the centre of a tooth, it causes terrible toothache.

Tooth decay does not hurt until it reaches the centre of a tooth, which is where the nerves are. When the decay reaches the nerves, the tooth throbs with pain.

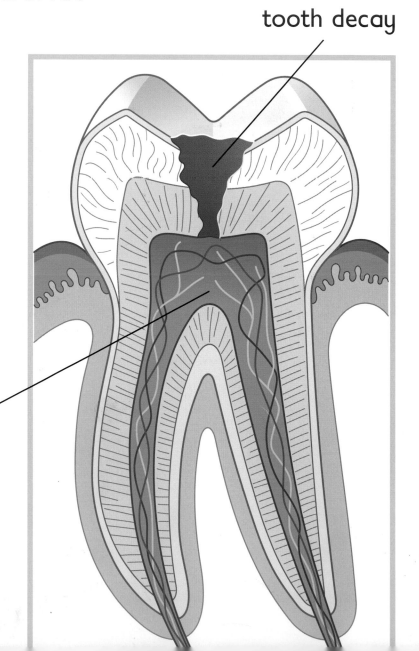

tooth decay

centre of tooth

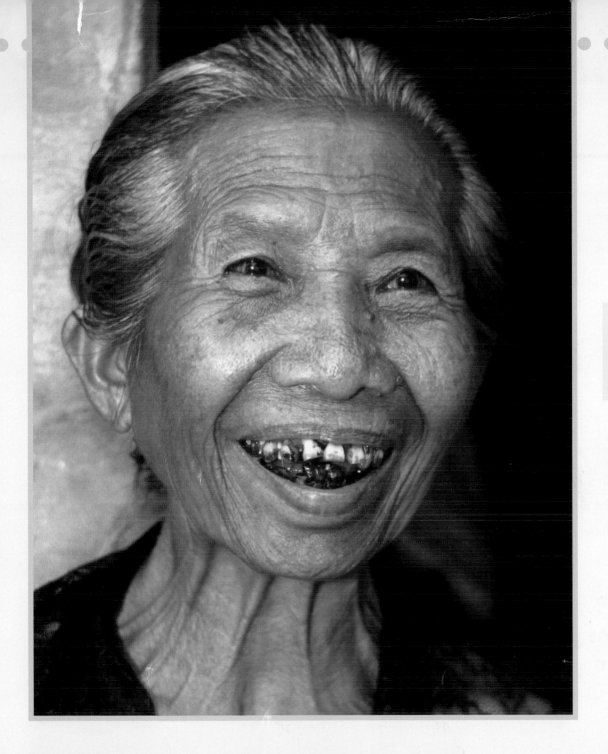

If tooth decay is not treated, the tooth
will die and go brown, like the teeth in this
photograph. If a tooth is badly damaged by
tooth decay, it may have to be pulled out.
If someone loses an adult tooth, it must
be replaced by a **false tooth**.

How do dentists treat tooth decay?

A dentist cleans away the **rotten** part of the tooth. He or she then fills the hole with special **chemicals**.

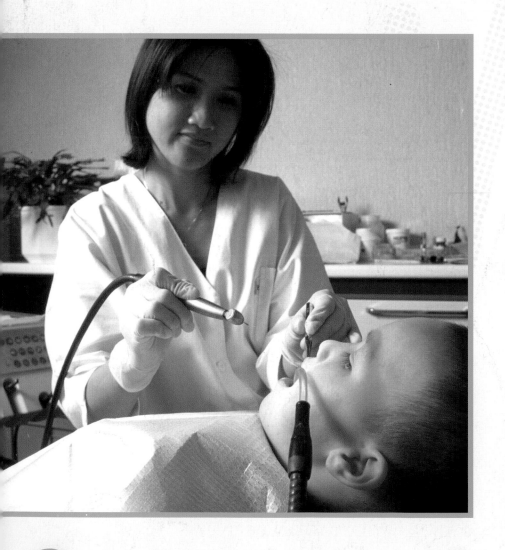

A dentist uses a drill to grind away all the rotting bits of the tooth. This makes the hole in the tooth even bigger!

The dentist cleans the hole and fills it. The filling is made of special chemicals that are very hard. Although the chemicals last a long time, nothing lasts as long as a natural tooth.

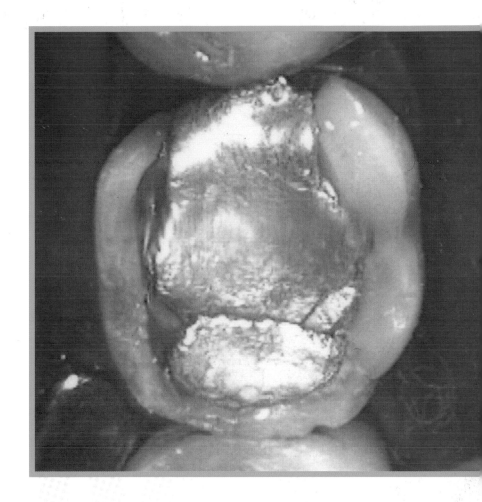

What are fillings made of?

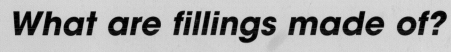

+ Dentists often use a silver filling for back teeth. This filling is a mixture of two **metals** – silver and **mercury**.
+ Dentists use white fillings for front teeth. This filling is made of very hard plastic mixed with glass.

15

How can you stop tooth decay?

The best way to avoid tooth decay is to clean your teeth well.

You should clean your teeth with toothpaste twice a day. Clean them last thing at night and then again in the morning, after you have eaten your breakfast.

How to clean your teeth:

1. Brush your teeth from the gums down to the tips of your teeth.
2. Brush the front of all your teeth, then brush the backs.
3. Brush the tops of the back teeth.

Do not keep a toothbrush until it is worn out. The bristles of a toothbrush should be straight and firm. If they are not they will not clean your teeth properly. You should get a new toothbrush every few months.

old toothbrush

new toothbrush

What is gum disease?

Gum disease is when the gums are **infected** by bacteria. Infected gums may bleed.

Plaque often forms between the teeth and the gums. The bacteria in the plaque can cause gum disease. Gums may then become sore and bleed.

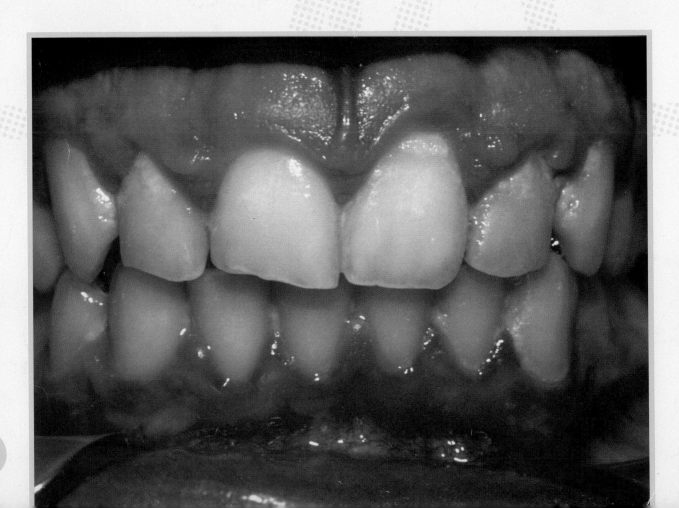

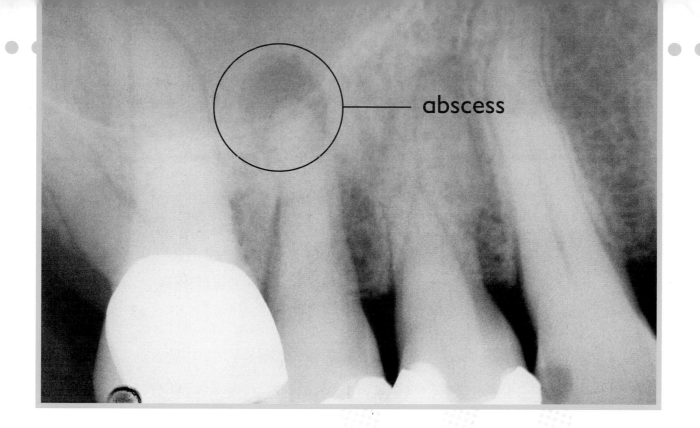

abscess

Sometimes gum disease causes a painful swelling called an **abscess**. The abscess forms around the tooth in the gum. The tooth becomes too sore to use.

Signs of gum disease:

+ Gums bleed when you brush your teeth.
+ Gums are sore and swollen.
+ Your breath smells bad.

How is gum disease treated?

A **mouthwash** can be used to treat mild gum disease.

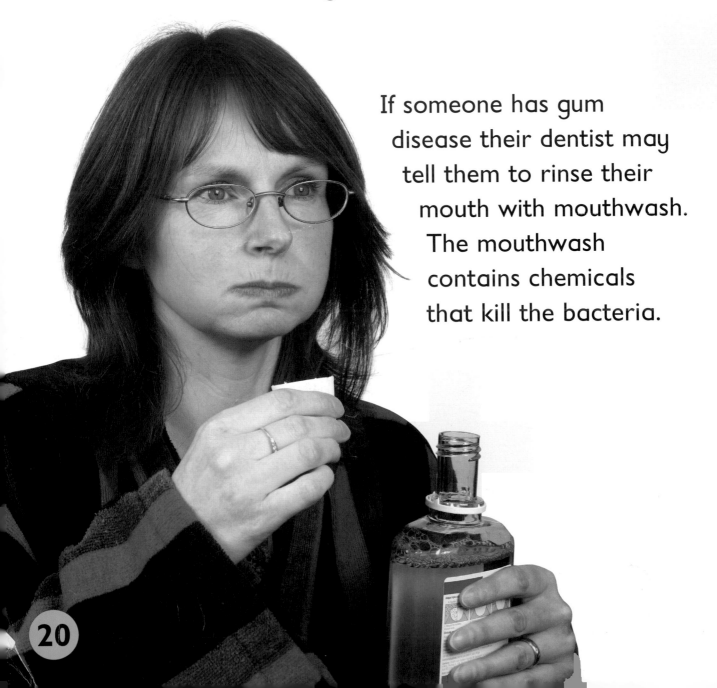

If someone has gum disease their dentist may tell them to rinse their mouth with mouthwash. The mouthwash contains chemicals that kill the bacteria.

If someone has an abscess they will need a stronger medicine than mouthwash. A doctor or dentist will give them an **antibiotic** medicine to kill the bacteria.

Take care!

+ Never take medicine unless an adult gives it to you. Do not take medicine that is meant for someone else.
+ Follow the instructions for an antibiotic medicine carefully.
+ You may still need to take the medicine after the abscess stops hurting.

21

How can you prevent gum disease?

Dental floss helps to clean away the plaque that causes gum disease.

Dental floss is a special thread that cleans away hidden plaque. It reaches plaque between the teeth and under the gums.

Dental check-ups

Regular dental check-ups help to prevent gum disease and tooth decay. During a check-up a dentist:

+ Checks for tooth decay and gum disease.
+ Checks that your teeth are straight.
+ May show you the right way to clean your teeth.
+ May seal your teeth with a special chemical. The seal makes it harder for tooth decay to start.

People usually floss their teeth before they clean them with a toothbrush. This lifts out any plaque from between the teeth and gums so it can be brushed away.

Which foods and drinks harm teeth?

Sweet snacks and sweet drinks are bad for your teeth.

Sweet foods contain a lot of sugar. If you eat them, sugar will be left in your mouth. If you do eat sweet foods, have them only once or twice a day.

Sweet drinks like these coat your teeth with a layer of sugar. Sweet drinks cause plaque more easily than sweet food.

Which foods and drink are good for teeth?

Eating cheese and vegetables and drinking water help to keep your teeth healthy.

A drink of water helps to wash away any sugar left in your mouth. Have a drink of water after you have eaten or drunk something sweet. Eating healthy foods that contain vitamin C, such as fruit and vegetables, will also keep your gums healthy.

Eating raw vegetables and fruit, such as apples, helps to clean your teeth. Some foods, such as cheese and yogurt, contain a **mineral** called **calcium**. Your teeth need calcium to grow.

Foods that contain calcium:

+ Milk and cheese.
+ Yogurt.
+ Sardines.
+ **Tofu**.
+ Almonds.
+ White bread.
+ Watercress.

Glossary

abscess swollen area of gum that has been infected by bacteria.

acid liquid that can burn holes in materials.

antibiotic medicine that kills bacteria.

bacteria tiny living things that can cause disease.

calcium mineral that makes your teeth and bones strong and hard.

canine pointed tooth.

chemical a powerful substance found in many man-made things, including fillings and mouthwash.

dentine hard part of a tooth between the centre and the enamel.

disclosure tablet tablet that shows up plaque in your mouth.

enamel very hard outer layer of a tooth.

false tooth artificial tooth made by a dentist.

gum pink flesh that covers the roots of your teeth.

incisor sharp, flat tooth at the front of the mouth.

infected affected by bacteria or other disease.

magnified made to look much bigger.

mercury special kind of metal that is mixed with silver to make a tooth filling.

metal substance, normally mined from the ground, that can be melted and made into different shapes.

mineral substance found in some foods. The body needs minerals to stay healthy.

molar large, bumpy tooth at the back of the mouth.

mouthwash   liquid for cleaning the mouth.

nerve   part of the body that carries messages to and from the brain.

plaque sticky paste made of bacteria that causes tooth decay.

premolar small molar.

rotten broken down by bacteria.

tofu   food made from soya beans.

Find out more

Find out about about tooth decay:
www.kidshealth.org/kid/talk/qa/cavity.html

Learn about going to the dentist and how to clean and floss your teeth:
www.kidshealth.org/kid/feel_better/
people/go_dentist.html

Index

abscess 19, 21
acid 10, 11
antibiotic 21

bacteria 10–11, 18, 20–21
bad breath 19
brushing teeth 7, 11, 16–17,
     19, 23

calcium 27
canines 9
chemicals 14–16, 16, 20

dentine 8
dentists 14–15, 20, 23
disclosure tablets 11
drinks 7, 10, 24–25, 26

enamel 8

false teeth 13
fillings 14–15
flossing 22–23
foods 7, 9, 10, 24–25, 26–27

gum disease 18–19, 20–21,
     22–23
gums 9, 17, 18–19, 22–23

incisors 9

medicines 21
mercury 15
milk teeth 9
molars 9
mouthwash 20–21

nerves 8, 12

plaque 10–11, 18, 22–23, 25
premolars 9

silver 15
sugar 10–11, 24–25, 26
sweets 7, 24–25

toothache 7, 12
toothbrushes 17, 23
tooth decay 6–7, 10–11,
     12–13, 14–15, 16–17, 23
toothpaste 16